BUILDING AN
AIRPLANE

BY DANIELLE S. HAMMELEF

CONTENT CONSULTANT
RYAN P. STARKEY, PH.D.
DEPT. OF AEROSPACE
ENGINEERING SCIENCES
UNIVERSITY OF COLORADO, BOULDER

READING CONSULTANT
BARBARA J. FOX
PROFESSOR EMERITA
NORTH CAROLINA STATE UNIVERSITY

CAPSTONE PRESS
a capstone imprint

Blazers Books are published by Capstone Press,
1710 Roe Crest Drive, North Mankato, Minnesota 56003
www.capstonepub.com

Library of Congress Cataloging-in-Publication Data
Cataloging-in-publication information is on file with the Library of Congress.

ISBN 978-1-4765-3978-2 (library binding)
ISBN 978-1-4765-5118-0 (paperback)
ISBN 978-1-4765-5959-9 (eBook)

Editorial Credits
Mandy Robbins, editor; Kyle Grenz, designer; Kathy McColley, production specialist

Photo Credits
Alamy: Bill Bachmann, 13, Chico Sanchez, 22, Itar-Tass Photo Agency, 19, PF-(mil2), 21; Getty Images: AFP/Pascal Pavani, 28-29; Newscom: Deutsch Presse Agentur/Maurizio Gambarini, 26, Itar-Tass Photos/Lystseva Marina, 14-15; Science Source, 8, James King-Holmes, 7, 10, Maximilian Stock Ltd, 16-17, Reporters/John Thys, 25; Shutterstock: Christopher Parypa, 4-5, Igor Marx, cover (airplane), Khafizov Ivan Harisovich, 1, Nikkolia, cover, 1 (inset laser), Saulius L, cover (engine), sparkdesign, throughout (background)

Printed in the United States of America.
2894

TABLE OF CONTENTS

ONE PLANE, MILLIONS OF PARTS

Look up! In the United States, nearly 9 million planes soar through the sky every year. Before an airplane takes off, hundreds of people work to make millions of parts fit together. How do they build a giant metal machine that flies through the sky?

In 2012 United States airlines carried about 642 million passengers.

CHAPTER 2

DESIGNING AND TESTING PLANES

Engineers study how planes move through the air. They compare types of wings, tails, and **fuselages** before making new designs. Other team members create computer images of the designs and build **scale** models.

engineer—a person who uses science and math to plan, design, or build

fuselage—the main body of an airplane

scale—describes something that is built with the same proportions of something else but at a different size

FACT
On December 17, 1903, Orville and
Wilbur Wright flew the first airplane.
Their first flight lasted 12 seconds.

Computers show how air will flow around a plane. ▼

Before building full-sized planes, engineers test their models. They run computer programs to see how the planes will fly in cold, hot, wet, or dry weather. Engineers also test their models in wind tunnels.

FACT
Workers test planes with wingspans up to 100 feet (30 meters) inside the world's largest wind tunnel in California.

wind tunnel—a tunnel through which air is blown to study airflow around an object

Engineers use the test results to reshape the plane's wings, tail, and fuselage. These changes smooth airflow around the plane. Once their model plans are approved, engineers send their designs to airplane parts factories.

MAKING PLANE PARTS

Different factories make different plane parts. Workers fit plastic and **carbon fiber** sheets around strong frames to build parts of the fuselage. They join the sheets to the frame with melted metal and pins.

carbon fiber—a strong, lightweight material used to make airplanes

Wings must be strong to withstand high-speed flight. They must also be lightweight to lift off the ground. Workers use aluminum or carbon fiber to build the wings. These strong, lightweight materials are perfect for the job.

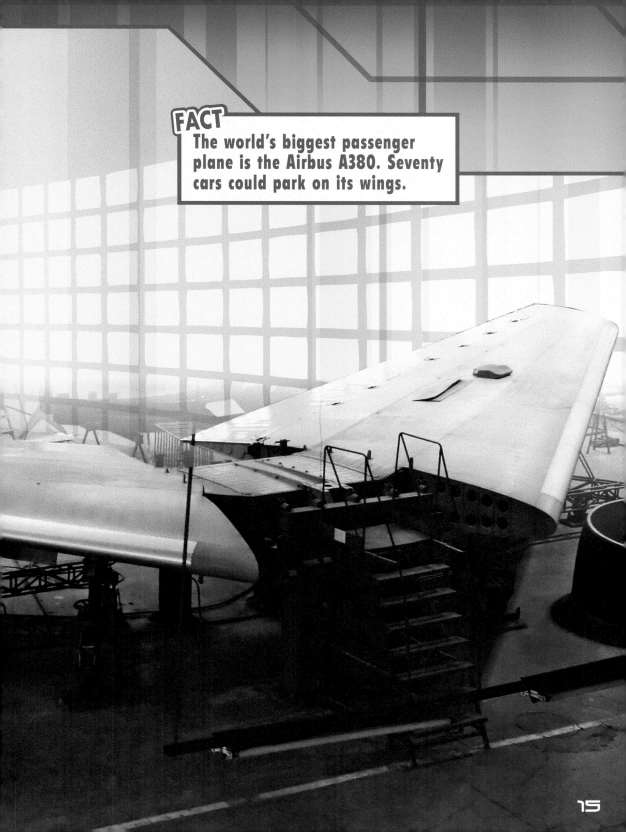

FACT

The world's biggest passenger plane is the Airbus A380. Seventy cars could park on its wings.

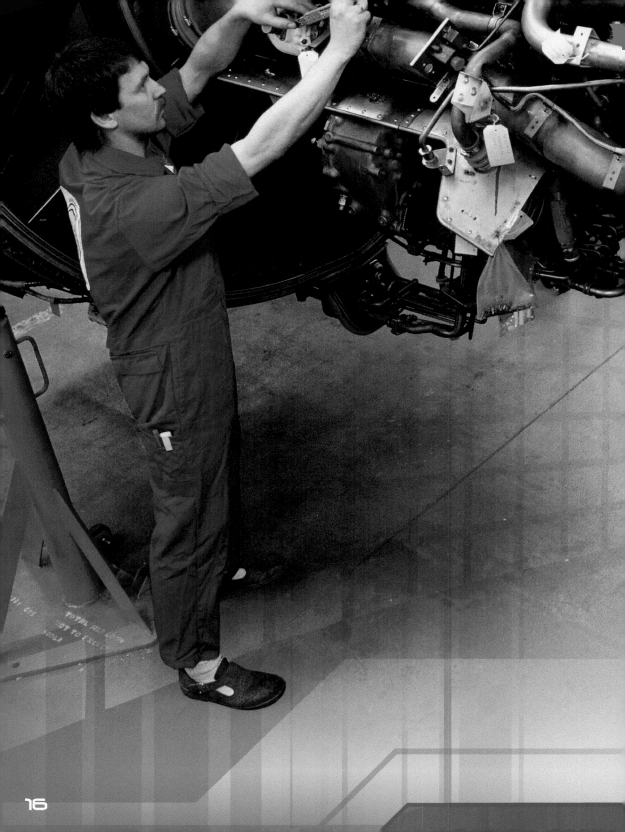

Other factories build engines. They use materials such as ceramics. Temperatures in an engine can reach 4,892 degrees Fahrenheit (2,700 degrees Celsius). Ceramics hold up in high heat.

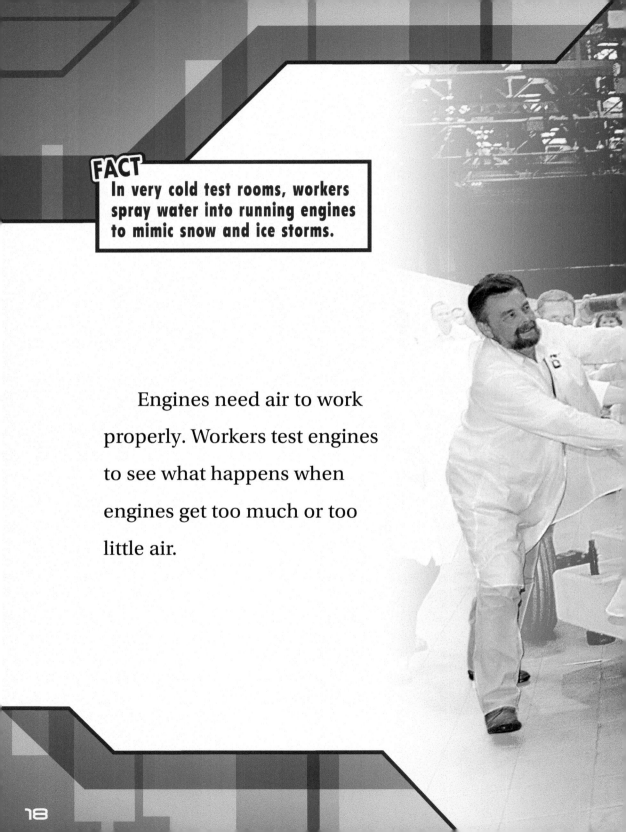

In very cold test rooms, workers spray water into running engines to mimic snow and ice storms.

Engines need air to work properly. Workers test engines to see what happens when engines get too much or too little air.

CHAPTER 4

AT THE ASSEMBLY PLANT

Cargo planes, trains, trucks, and ships take parts to the assembly plant. First workers connect the fuselage pieces. Then robots help workers join the wings, tail sections, and landing gear to the fuselage.

FACT
Trucks move the Airbus A380's parts at night. One French town widened its streets and cut down trees so that trucks hauling parts could get through.

Depending on the plane, workers thread up to 330 miles (531 kilometers) of wires through the plane's frame. The wires bring electricity all over the airplane. Lights, cockpit instruments, and refrigerators all run on electricity.

FACT
Bad electrical wiring is a common cause of airplane fires. Electrical wiring must be installed properly to prevent these fires.

cockpit—the area in the front of a plane where the pilot sits

Workers pull the plane to the painting booth. Painters spray-paint the airplane with the airline's colors and logos. Teams of eight people can paint a passenger plane in about three days.

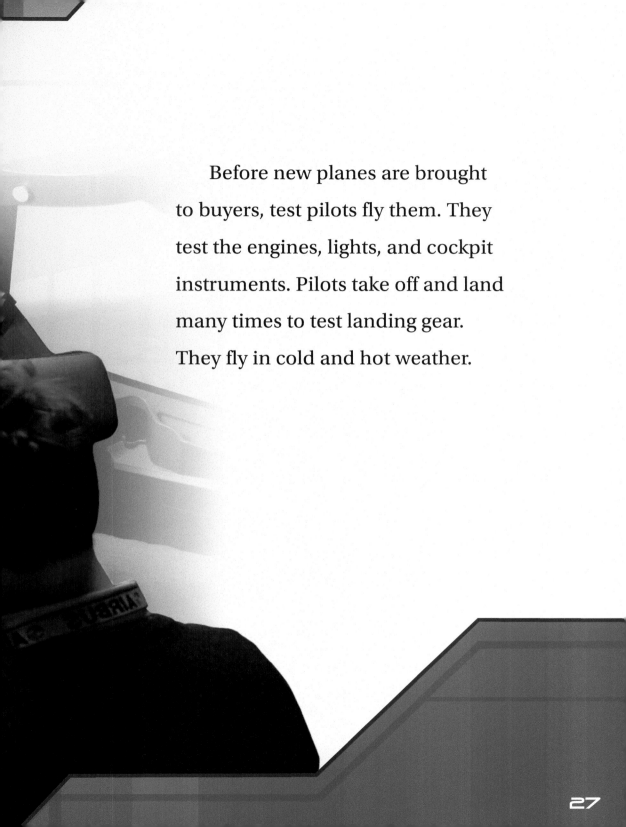

Before new planes are brought to buyers, test pilots fly them. They test the engines, lights, and cockpit instruments. Pilots take off and land many times to test landing gear. They fly in cold and hot weather.

CHAPTER 5

DELIVERING COMPLETED PLANES

Delivery teams fly the finished plane to its buyers. The teams teach new owners about the airplane. **Commercial** planes can now take off, carrying people and cargo around the world. Military planes roam the skies to protect and serve their nations.

commercial—suitable for business use, rather than private use

FACT
In 2012 airlines in the United States used more than 14.7 billion gallons (55.6 billion liters) of fuel.

GLOSSARY

carbon fiber (KAHR-buhn FY-buhr)—a strong, lightweight material used to make airplanes

cargo (KAHR-goh)—the goods carried by a ship, vehicle, or aircraft

ceramic (sayr-AM-ic)—an object made of clay

cockpit (KOK-pit)—the area in the front of a plane where the pilot sits

commercial (kuh-MUHR-shuhl)—suitable for business use, rather than private use

engineer (en-juh-NEER)—a person who uses science and math to plan, design, or build

fuselage (FYOO-suh-lahzh)—the main body of an airplane

robot (ROH-bot)—a machine that is programmed to do jobs that are usually performed by a person

scale (SKALE)—describes something that is built with the same proportions of something else but at a different size

wind tunnel (WIND TUH-nuhl)—a tunnel through which air is blown to study airflow around an object

READ MORE

Doman, Mary Kate. *Airplanes*. All About Big Machines. Berkeley Heights, N.J.: Enslow Elementary, 2012.

Glaser, Rebecca Stromstad. *Airplanes.* Machines at Work. Minneapolis: Jump!, 2013.

Ohmann, Paul. *How Airplanes Work.* Mankato, Minn.: Child's World, 2012.

Schaefer, Lola M. *Airplanes in Action.* Transportation Zone. North Mankato, Minn.: Capstone Press, 2012.

INTERNET SITES

FactHound offers a safe, fun way to find Internet sites related to this book. All of the sites on FactHound have been researched by our staff.

Here's all you do:

Visit *www.facthound.com*

Type in this code: 9781476539782

 Check out projects, games and lots more at
www.capstonekids.com

INDEX